Life should be an adventure. Life should be fulfilling.
Life should be more than simply existing.

START
SUCCEEDING

MINDSET
GOALS
PLANS

The Three Key Ingredients to Achieving Your Success

RANDY W. DRAKE
with Craig Alan Clark

The Randy Drake Team
1194 Knight Trail
Milton ON L9T 5R9
www.randydraketeam.com

Ordering Information:
Quantity sales. Special discounts are available on quantity purchases
by corporations, associations, and others. For details, contact the pub-
lisher at the address above.

ISBN 978-0-9953210-0-7

Printed in Canada

This book is dedicated to my Family:

My wife, Nancy, who has been with me for the past 31 years

Our two sons, Tyler and Sean.

To my Mother, whom I miss every day

To my Father, who told me once, "the day we stop dreaming is the day we die." I am still dreaming Dad!

To Katelyn, for being my Superstar student.

FOREWORD

I first met Randy Drake back in late 2014 via a mastermind and training program we both were participating in. He was a technical and project management specialist, in his "day job," and hadn't yet begun his career in coaching, teaching, and training. His keen eye for emerging trends in his community and general geographic area impressed me—and it wasn't long before I was amazed that, unlike so many others he started having great ideas AND quickly taking action on them.

As co-trainees and mastermind partners both of us were focusing on our individual businesses while still sharing valuable insights with one another and others that were a part of the group seem to be a bit distracted and not moving forward with their business ideas. Whereas many were taking a one size fits all approach to their entrepreneurial dreams. Randy was looking for ways to better understand and meet his markets expectations.

In mid-2015 Randy had an idea to launch his first live event that focused on an individual's ability step out and pursued their dreams of success. He enlisted other smart people like himself who could add value to the attendees, and after learning as he went along, he launched his first live event. Did I mention it was a rousing success?! Thanks to Randy and his team being true to their purpose.

START SUCCEEDING Mindset • Goals • Plans: The Three Key Ingredients to Achieving Success is not only his first book but also a wake-up call for anyone who is ready to take action on pursuing his or her success. Despite the fact, many may be bewildered with the myriad of choices out in the marketplace they should start with Randy Drake's new little book that is full of some enormous lessons on success.

Theodore Henderson, Owner and Founder
TheodoreHenderson.com, LaunchingYourGreatBusinessIdeaNow.
com
Best Selling Author of the Books
"9 Simple Strategies to Becoming a Strong Leader"
"The Wisdom Compass For Business: Your 8 Keys to Real Success"
"The Wisdom Compass: A 31-day Journey To Wisdom Filled Living"

TABLE OF CONTENTS

INTRODUCTION

Every day you see people that are successful and happy. They are working at jobs or careers they love. They have strong relationships with family and friends. You see them having fun and doing all the things you wish you could do. It looks like they must know something you don't. Some sort of secret allowing them to live a life of success.

Well, what if I told you that you could learn these secrets. That you too can have what these successful people have. That if you follow the steps in this book you can change the results in your life and move towards everything you want.

Happy, healthy and wealthy individuals are definitely not lucky. They have made a conscious decision to achieve their goals. Something I hope you will make here and now. If you want to be successful, you must make a permanent decision. A decision to choose to get what you want out of life while still respecting the rights of others

Over the past 20 years, I have been studying why people are successful and others not. Investigating why some get all the breaks and others fail no matter what.

When I was in school, I was under the perception that hard work and education was the key to wealth. However, I watched my father work hard his whole life. He had a loving wife and four children. We had food on the table, a roof over our heads, he always had a job, but not a lot of money. We never went on extravagant family vacations. There were Christmases with not many presents under the tree. He worked very hard for what he had, but never became wealthy.

Was this *his* dream, *his* goal in life? Or did he *want* more? He once told me, "the day we stop dreaming is the day we die."

So what makes a person successful? What makes a person feel as if they are accomplishing something? How do you find your purpose in life? How do you follow your passion? These are the questions that I wanted to be answered.

What was the answer? And how could I learn the secret? I have read numerous books. Such as *Think and Grow Rich*, *The Science of Getting Rich*, *As a man Thinketh*, *The Power of the Sub-Conscious Mind*, *The 21 Irrefutable Laws of Leadership*, and many more. I have trained under experts in leadership and business. Experts such as John Maxwell, Bob Proctor, Darren Hardy, Jim Rohn and others. Through this self-development,

I finally discovered what it took to be successful. This book is a summary of what I have learned over those years and what I now teach others in their pursuit of success.

I will cover your six intellectual faculties:

- Imagination
- Intuition
- Will
- Memory
- Reason
- Perception

You will learn the importance your Mindset, Goals and Plans have on the results you are achieving.

We will cover:

- Attitude
- Paradigms
- Terror Barriers
- Affirmations
- Creating Goals
- Visualization
- and much more...

CHAPTER 1

KATE'S STORY: THE WOMAN WITHOUT A DREAM

"Reach high for stars lie hidden in your soul. Dream deep, for every dream precedes the goal."

Pamela Vauli Star

To help explain the ideas and lessons in this book we will be following the journey taken by a young woman named Kate. I had the privilege of training and coaching her on the journey to success.

I've known Kate most of her life, her parents are good friends of mine. By the age of 24, Kate had attended one semester of university. After she started attending classes the subjects she chose to study, Philosophy, had no appeal to her. So, she decided to leave and pursue something else, something that might interest her. She had always loved art. In High School, she enjoyed painting and creating abstract pictures. She painted for her own enjoyment for a few years, but did not believe there was any possible way to make a living doing it. One of Kate's friends told her there was money to be made doing makeup application for people. She thought this would be a great way to use her love of painting to earn a living. She decided to enroll in college to become a makeup artist and was informed it would be best for her to take esthetician classes, as this would give her a better chance of finding a job after her graduation. She had been told a person that can do more than just makeup application is in a high demand.

Kate enjoyed her time at college. Learning new skills and especially her classes in makeup. She excelled in that class and was so happy she could use her love of art in a way to make her money. Upon graduating, she quickly got a job at a small hair salon and spa.

After six months of working at the salon, she came to the realization the job wasn't at all what she expected. She had envisioned herself applying makeup to clients making them look and feel beautiful. Instead, all they were interested in were manicures, pedicures and waxing. Before too long, Kate began to hate going to work, it would just be yet another day of nails and waxing.

She had no idea what she was supposed to do. She worked hard to become an esthetician only to realize once again she's unhappy. Kate felt lost with a sense of dread, with nothing to look forward to. She lived the way most people do following the crowd with no purpose in life. Trying to survive, just simply existing.

For years I had been going to the Salon and Spa Kate worked at. During my visits, I would talk about my business as a success coach and the programs I was designing to help people. The owner was very interested and wanted to learn more. She felt the training I was providing could help improve her and her business. So we worked out an agreement to beta test my program with her staff. This allowed me the opportunity to develop and fine tune it with them.

I had just finished one of these training sessions, a lesson I had developed based on a book by John Maxwell called "Putting Your Dream to the Test". The training was "the ten questions you should ask yourself when deciding on whether you should pursue a dream." The lesson went well with everyone, except Kate. When we had finished the training, Kate volunteered to stay back and lock up. She asked me if I had a minute to talk with her alone.

"Sure, what's on your mind?" I asked.

"Well," she began. "It's just that I enjoyed your training, but it made me realize something."

"What did it make you realize?" I inquired.

"It made me realize that I have no idea what my dream is," she said with a sad look on her face.

Kate was struggling with the concept of happiness. She knew she wasn't happy and believed it would naturally come later in life. Kate had no passions, interests or hobbies. Switched between multiple jobs. Just stuck in a chasm of the repeat work day. Knowing she had somewhere to be, but no idea of the reason why. She had dreams, but they faltered as she became an adult.

"You don't have a dream?" I asked. "What is it that you are passionate about? What do you want out of life? "

"I don't know. I don't know what my passion or my dream is in life. I don't know how to be successful." Kate replied.

It was clear to me she wanted more in her life. Working any longer at the salon was giving her anxiety. Kate was frustrated. This isn't what she imagined life would be. She had no clue how to figure it all out.

"I've watched you Randy, move up the corporate ladder and become very successful. I want what you have," she added.

"Kate, what are your life goals and your plans to achieve them?" I asked.

"I have no idea," she said. "I have no idea what my goal is or should be. And I have no idea how to get it!" she added in frustration.

"Kate, what do you want in life?"

"It doesn't matter what I want, it's not like I am going to get it." Kate snapped back.

"What is stopping you from having what you want?"

Kate started giving me what she believed were the reasons why she wasn't getting the results she wished for in life. Things like, the economy, no help from her friends nor her family, not being able to find the right job, and on and on.

"I'm simply not happy," she finally said. "And I don't know how to change it. My life sucks. I'm tired of simply existing. I want to learn how to be more. I want to start being successful!"

"Kate, let me explain something to you that will start helping you to become successful and achieve your dreams," I began. "The only thing that is responsible for the results you are getting in your life is you. Whatever you have been telling yourself will reflect in your results. If you think to yourself, it's impossible to accomplish my dream you may never achieve it. Your mind is very powerful and it will do everything it can to prove you right. So when you think or say that you can't do something your mind will go back into your memory and remind you of every time you failed. This way you will believe that if you couldn't do it in the past how is it possible for you to do it now."

"Wow," replied Kate, "I never realized that I was my own worst enemy! I always blamed others or my situation for why things aren't working out."

"Yes it is difficult to believe that we are in control of our results, but that is also very good." I added.

"It is?" asked Kate. "It sure is," I replied. "You see if you believe in your dreams, then all of the resources available will help you succeed. It is your habits and beliefs that cause you to act in a certain way. The way you act causes a reaction. And then that reaction gives you your results."

"So what you are telling me is that I have control over my own future?" She says in awe.

"That is exactly right. You must decide to make a change and learn to alter your habits and beliefs," I said. "Kate, life should be an adventure. Life should be fulfilling. Life should be more than simply existing. Most people are only experiencing a fraction of the joy and satisfaction that is available to them! If you wish to change, your life from simply existing to one that is successful; you will need to learn and understand these three key ingredients to achieving your success they are mindset, goals, and plans."

"What do you mean by mindset, goals and plans?" Kate

inquired.

Mindset is your Paradigm; this is a multitude of ideas, which are fixed, in your subconscious mind. These fixed ideas commonly referred to as your habits and beliefs. These habits and beliefs can act like blinders and can cause you to miss seeing opportunities, which are out there waiting for you. Mindset also covers your awareness. The awareness of how the mind works and how to use it to help you achieve your dreams. With a new mindset, you will want to act on the new opportunities you are seeing. To do this you need to learn how to set proper Goals. When you select the proper goal, every aspect of your life will improve because of the person you will become in achieving these goals. However, goals without plans are merely wishes. You need to develop plans to help you move towards your goals. Learn to make your decisions based on whether they move you closer to, or take you away from your goal.

"So how do I learn all of this? I'm tired of this life I am living. I'm tired of simply existing. I want more out of life."

"If you want to discover your passions and make your dreams come true you need to spend time with me," I responded. "During this time I will train, coach and mentor you through the process of success."

"So, I cannot be successful until I understand why I do what I do and know what I want to do with my life?" Kate asked as she started to become more interested in my concepts.

"Exactly," I told her. "How can you be successful if you don't know what you want? You must learn to understand yourself. You can achieve this by getting a clearer knowledge of your mind and determining its power. I will teach you how it works and how to use this power to achieve your dream," I said

"However, before you can become successful, you must have a clear definition of success. It's different for everyone. For some it means having money or power. For others a loving family, a beautiful home or a job you like."

"So, what is your definition of success?" Asked Kate

"The best definition I have been able to find goes like this. Success is the positive progression towards ones idea or goal." I told her.

A person who owns a café because that was their life goal is successful. A woman who is a mother because she wanted children is successful. An entrepreneur running a business because that was their dream is successful. Any person working in a positive progression towards their idea or goal is successful."

"So I need to have a dream to become successful?" asked Kate.

"Yes you do, but before that you need to understand the importance of awareness, your paradigm and how goals are used to work with the first two to achieve your dream."

"So when can we get started? Can you please teach me what I need to know so that I can make changes in my life? I really want to do this; I want to be happy and enjoy life." Kate pleaded to me.

"Yes I can teach you what you need to know to make the changes you are looking for in your life. However, you must promise me to take everything I teach you seriously. There will be some difficult decisions and work if you are going to change the results you are getting now." I told her sternly.

"I am ready." She replied. "I will do all the work, I promise. When do we start?"

"Take some time to think about all the things you have learned here," I said. "Next time we meet, I will be talking to you about attitude and its importance to being successful."

"I would like you to take some time and list out some of

the things that you want in your life. Not needs but wants. These will be used later to help you discover your dream and create your goal to achieve it."

"Thank you, I do have lots to think about," concluded Kate. "I still do not know my dream or what I really want in life. But, I understand I have lots to learn and work to do to make me successful."

"Great. I hope I haven't overwhelmed you." I said. "As we move forward through the training you will discover that everything will come together and make sense to you."

"I'm looking forward to it." Said Kate. "See you soon."

CHAPTER 2

THE IMPORTANCE OF A POSITIVE ATTITUDE

"Nothing can stop the man with the right mental attitude from achieving his goal; nothing on earth can help the man with the wrong mental attitude."

Thomas Jefferson

When Kate asked me how to discover her dream all she knew was that she was unhappy with the results in her life. I had informed her she would need to understand her life was a result of her mindset, goals and plans. She would need to learn about each of these key ingredients to success if she wanted to change her life. I decided the best way to introduce her to understanding mindset was to teach her first lesson on the importance of having a positive attitude.

Two weeks had passed. It was time to meet Kate and give her first lesson. We met at a coffee shop near her home. It was a fancy place with a huge menu of different drinks. I ordered us both large cappuccinos and found a quiet place to sit near the back. We sat there for a few minutes sipping our coffees when I decided it was time to break the silence.

"So Kate, do you have any question for me since our last meeting?" I began.

At the end of the last session I recommended she try different social activities. With a range of different skills and subjects. Kate told me she tried Cocktails and Canvas, a group painting night usually held in pub or bars. She was an extra in a music video, made friends and had fun. But, she was still discovering her passions.

"Well, you gave me lots to think about and I realize now that if I want to improve my life that I need to improve myself first," Kate responded.

"Exactly, excellent way to say it" Kate gave me a funny little smile. "What are you thinking?" I probed.

"Well, you use that word a lot," she said.

"What word?" I asked.

"Excellent," she said. "Whenever I ask you how you are, you always tell me you are excellent. How can you always be excellent, there must be days when you are not excellent?"

"Now, it is interesting that you should ask me about my attitude today Kate," I continued, "Today's lesson is on the importance of having a positive attitude. My attitude is my choice therefore; I choose to be excellent."

You may not realize it but your attitude towards life has a large impact on the results you are getting. A positive attitude moves us towards success. All through your life, the importance of having a positive attitude has been stressed upon you. In your classroom, teachers would tell you to have a good attitude and it will help you get better grades. On your sports team, the coach would tell you and your team mates how important attitude is whether you win or lose. At your workplace, a positive attitude can be the difference between getting a promotion and being over looked for a promotion.

There has been plenty of studies on the lives of the successful. A recent study at Stanford University by Psychologist Carol Dweck shows that your attitude is a better predictor of your success than your IQ.

According to Shawn Achor, Harvard researcher and positive psychology expert, predicting an employee's future success at a company has traditionally stumped experts, and relying on metrics such as IQ level, which only tells 25% of the story. What makes up the other 75% is the person's attitude.

Positive individuals expect nothing but success. You can spot them as they walk into a room. They have a presence you can feel. Successful people all have their attitude in common. They are positive people. They are all aware of their potential and understand how to develop it.

"What do you mean your attitude is your choice?" Kate asked. "Doesn't your circumstances and what is happening around you determine your attitude?"

"You see everything just is until we decide what it is," I said.

"What?" she interjected

"Well, let me try to explain," I continued, "until you make a decision about something it is neither good nor bad, it just is."

"How does that work?"

Now to develop a positive attitude you must first understand your attitude is a choice and not something that happens to you or caused by outside forces. You have complete control on whether your attitude is positive or negative. To understand this you must first understand what makes it up. Your attitude is a combination of three things, your thoughts, feelings and actions. This combination determines whether we have a positive or negative attitude. If you change your thinking, but your feelings and actions remain the same then your attitude will not suddenly be positive. It's the same for any formulation of these qualities. You need to understand these three parts and how to make a unified change.

THOUGHTS are your reasoning mind. What you think and believe to be true. However, most people never really take the time to think. Take a moment right now to think. Most people live their lives following the rest of the crowd. If the masses say something is good, then they believe it is good. If the masses say that it is bad then it must be bad. No one has ever stood out by following the crowd.

FEELINGS are your emotional mind. Your paradigm is the beliefs and habits that determine how you feel about ideas and things that happen in your life. It is through emotions most people make their decisions and act the way they do.

ACTIONS are what the outer world sees. They are the results of your thoughts and feelings. This is the direct connection between your mind and the physical world. Your results in life are of your actions and reactions they cause around you. The only way you can improve is to take full responsibility for your attitude.

I continued, "well let me explain it to you with a short story and see if that helps you to understand what I mean."

"Ok" Kate said.

A few years ago, my son Tyler was in a car accident. He had been out with friends and it was late in the evening. He had fallen asleep while driving home and came out of his lane hitting the car beside him. Both cars sustained minor damage as a result.

The phone rang and woke me up out of a deep sleep.

I answered it and Tyler explained to me what happened. He

was upset and scared. He had never been in an accident before and wasn't sure what he should do.

I had to make a decision. Would I see the entire negative side of the incident? Such as, an increase in his insurance cost, the cost of repairs to his car or the accident going onto his driving record. I could become upset and yell at my son for being irresponsible. Or, I could focus on the positive. My son was not hurt, the person he hit was fine and the cars were both repairable. I could be positive and calm to help my son through the experience.

It was my choice.

So, when he told me what happened, my choice could alter my response and outcome to the situation. Anyone can choose whether to have a positive or negative attitude towards things. I chose the positive attitude. I was grateful that he was fine and that no one was hurt.

You develop or choose your attitude and there is no one who can change it for you. Only you have the power to change it. Compare your Attitude to steering a car. Your steering determines your direction. If you want to go from Toronto to Montreal, you will only make it there by correctly directing your car. However, if you steer a little to the left you could end up in Ottawa.

The smallest change in your attitude can dramatically affect your future destination. It is up to you to decide whether to end up in Montreal or Ottawa.

A negative attitude keeps you from achieving your dreams. It blinds you from seeing possibilities and opportunities. It can drive helpful people away and attract the wrong ones. People with negative attitudes are drawn to each other.

Have you ever heard the expression birds of a feather flock together? Well it is true. In the book, "The Secret" Rhonda Byrne explains "The Law of Attraction." Like attracts like. So negative people attract negative people.

Your thinking must be of the negative bias for you to have a negative attitude. You tell yourself that nothing ever works out for you. You only see the obstacles in your way and all the issues there are in the world. Thinking this way causes you to have emotions of stress, anxiety and fear. They are all negative emotions. These transmit in your daily actions - causing you to send out negative vibes to the universe. Now your actions cause reactions from everyone you interact with giving you your results.

"Do you see now that the situation was neither positive

nor negative until I decided what it was?" I said.

"Yes! It makes sense now," she says with her wide eyes. "But is it always that easy?"

"I never said it was easy," I corrected her. "You will learn, life is much happier when you decide to be positive instead of negative. When you have a choice, why would you ever chose negative?"

"Virtually nothing is impossible in this world if you just put your mind to it and maintain a positive attitude," said former American football player and head coach at The College of William & Mary, North Carolina State University, the University of Notre Dame Lou Holtz. It is this ability to stay positive that will help you move towards success.

I see people every day who decide to be negative and go through life miserable and unhappy. They see what is wrong or negative in everything they do and with everyone, they meet. These would be the people who complain about how hard and how unfair life is. If only they could realized that if they made the choice to be positive, things could be so much better." I added.

"If they decided to be positive, everything would magically get better for them?" Kate asked.

"There is nothing magical about it, Kate. Once you make the decision to be positive, you will be surprised on how things around you begin to be positive." I explained. "Do you remember what I told you about the Law of Attraction?" I asked, "The universe will work to attract more positive things to you."

A positive attitude will do the opposite of a negative attitude. It attracts positive people who can help achieve your dreams. You will be open to suggestions and willing to learn. Thinking positively you now see possibilities and opportunities. You will have emotions of joy, calmness and reassurance. These positive emotions will send out positive vibes to the universe, bringing you positive results.

"Kate, I noticed your attitude can be very negative at times," I pointed out to her, though I can tell that it was hard for her to hear.

"You have a tendency of blaming others or your present situation and all the problems in your life. You need to take responsibility for your life." I said firmly to her.

"I don't control everything that is happening to me," Kate got defensive.

Looking straight into her eyes, I said, "no, you don't control EVERYTHING, but you do control your response to them. Let me put it this way: there is only one person who can change the results you are getting. There is only one person who can make you happy. There is only one person that is responsible for deciding your outlook on life. That person is you!"

Kate looked at me intently trying to figure everything out. As she sipped her drink, there was a small glimmer of understanding beginning to develop in the dark corner of the coffee shop.

"You must understand that you are in full control of your life, the results, and your happiness. You MUST know that three qualities make up your attitude: your thoughts, your feelings, and your actions. This combination, even with a slight change of them, can make a large impact on your results."

We all have a choice. Whether to have a positive or negative attitude. Whichever one we decide to take on, we must understand that the Law of Attraction is at work and we will attract to us more of what we have chosen.

The only person who can control your attitude is you. You are in control of your results.

"So Kate, the way you think about the things that happen

in your life, the way you feel about them, and the actions you take determine your attitude. You need to start thinking positively, feeling positive and acting positive." I said.

"How do I do that?" She says as she looks for more answers from me.

"That will be your next lesson," I said, holding her in suspense. "For the next little while, I have something I want you to do. Are you up for a challenge?"

"Yes, sure, I guess," Kate replied.

"For the next few weeks, I want you to take notice of your attitude and try to see the positive in every situation. Can you do that?" I asked.

"I will try my best." She said eagerly.

"Excellent!" I replied. We both looked at each other and laughed.

"I meant to say 'good'. Do your best and see what changes happen in your life."

CHAPTER 3

UNDERSTANDING THE THREE PARTS OF YOUR ATTITUDE (CONSCIOUS MIND, SUBCONSCIOUS MIND AND BODY)

"For success, attitude is equally as important as ability."

Walter Scott

To choose your attitude, you must first learn the three parts that create it. These are the same three parts that make up the MIND. When I say MIND, I am not speaking of your brain. The brain is a magnificent transmission and receiving center. A remarkable nerve center that sends electrical signals all over the body. When I talk about the MIND, I am referring to it as an ACTIVITY - your spirit or spiritual representation.

The Mind consists of three distinct parts, the Conscious Mind, the Subconscious Mind and the Body. You will learn how each of these parts work together to create your attitude. As I pointed out in the last chapter your attitude consist of the way you think, the Conscious Mind; the way you feel, the Subconscious Mind; and your actions, your Body. Once you understand how the mind works, you will be able to be able to choose your attitude.

After our last meeting at the coffee shop, I recommended Kate take some time to think seriously about her attitude and start to figure out her representation of thoughts, feelings, and actions. A couple weeks later, I met Kate at her work. We continued our lessons in the back room of the salon.

"So, Kate how have things been?" I asked. "Have you

tried being more positive?"

"I have so much to tell you," she said excitedly, "I have taken your advice and decided to be positive. What a difference! The other day, at work, it was a slow shift. There was nothing to do, so they sent me home for the afternoon. In the past, I would have been upset and negative. I'd wondering how I could afford to make my rent or cover my bills. This time, I decided to look for the positives.

It happened to be an unusually sunny and warm day for this time of year," she continued, "I decided to walk the steps of my apartment building for a workout."

I could see the positivity in her face. Her eyes were beaming with excitement at the changes she made.

"When I got to the top of the stairs, I came to the door that leads to the roof. Ordinarily, the doors would be locked, but today, the door was propped open." She continued, "So, I decided to get my neighbour and asked him if he wanted to join me on the rooftop for a chat. We talked and the afternoon melted away in the sun."

I could tell that my lessons were starting to make an impact on her life. I was proud that she was starting to make these connections. Kate was taking it seriously, and it was changing her attitude towards life.

"My neighbour looked over at me," continued Kate, "he said 'there is something different about you, I just cannot put my finger on it. I know what it is, you look happy. You are smiling. I don't usually see you smile. It's pretty. You should smile more often!'

Just by changing my attitude, my whole day got better. I'm going to try my hardest to be positive from now on."

"I am so proud of you Kate. That story is wonderful. I was hoping you would see the benefits of a positive attitude and you certainly did that." I said with a huge smile on my face. "Now when I last was with you I told you that I would explain the three parts that make up your attitude in more detail. Well it just so happens that these three parts are also the parts that create your Mind." "My Mind." Kate asked. "Yes that's correct your Mind" I answered.

"When I ask you to think of the MIND, what picture do you see?" I asked.

"I picture a brain," replied Kate.

"A brain is not your mind. The brain is a marvelous receiving and transmission station, but it is not the mind," I replied. "Mind is an ACTIVITY."

To understand the MIND, you must have an image of it. Humans think in pictures. If I were to say think of a car, you would pull up a picture of your car in your mind. You would not see the letters C-A-R, no you would see your car as a picture. Alternatively, if I say think of a house, you would think of a picture of your house.

In 1934, Dr. Thurman Fleet developed a model of the mind called The Stickperson. It is an extremely simple concept. The Stickperson consists of three parts: The Conscious Mind, the Subconscious Mind and the Body. Let me draw a picture of it for you so that you can get a better idea of what I am talking about.

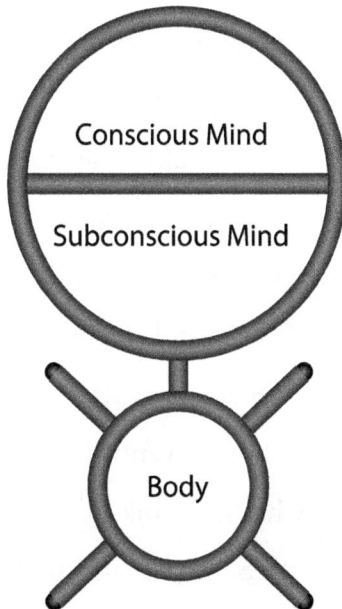

Conscious Mind

Subconscious Mind

Body

The Conscious Mind is the part of the MIND that thinks and reasons. It contains your free will. The Conscious Mind can accept or reject any idea introduced to it. It is with this part of your MIND that you can choose negative or positive thoughts. It is vital to understand you are in complete control of what you think. If you choose to think negatively about things, it is your choice and no one else's. You must learn to take responsibility for the way you think and understand you are the only one who can control it.

Your Conscious Mind is connected to your five senses: Seeing, Hearing, Touching, Tasting and Smelling. We are trained to use these senses exclusively for creating ideas. Most people make all of their decisions based on these five sensory factors. I call them outside forces.

You also have six mental faculties used to create ideas. Many fail to utilize them properly. These are your Imagination, Intuition, Will, Memory, Reason, and Perception. You have information coming from outside forces or internal thoughts. You can choose to either accept or reject them.

The thoughts you choose eventually determine your life results. You become what you think. This relates to the second part of the Stickman the Subconscious Mind. It is certainly the

38

most magnificent. It is the power center. It functions in every cell of your body, controls the respiratory system, keeps your heart beating, fights off infection, or heals a cut. Every thought your Conscious Mind chooses to accept, your Subconscious Mind must also accept. It has no ability to reject anything. It has no sense of humor, no knowledge of right and wrong, or good and bad. Your Subconscious Mind expresses itself through your feelings and actions.

Anything the Conscious Mind repeatedly impresses upon, the Subconscious Mind must accept it. Whatever it is given will become fixed in your paradigm. Until they are replaced, fixed ideas will continue to express themselves without conscious assistance. We refer to these fixed ideas as habits and beliefs. We use these every day in our lives. Most of the time we use them without even realizing it.

THINK about learning to drive a car. At first, you pay attention to every detail such as how hard to press the gas pedal and how soon to start braking. After doing it repeatedly, it becomes a habit. As an experienced driver, you make all of those decisions without putting in much thought. They are habits controlled by the Subconscious Mind. The Subconscious Mind also works as a powerful search engine. When you ask it a question, it will look everywhere it can to find you the answer.

"Kate if you think it is impossible to achieve your dream, your Subconscious Mind will do everything it can to prove you right, It will bring up memories of every time in the past you failed." I said to Kate as we continued our conversation. "It wants to prove you right. You will remember all your past defeats and conclude there is no sense trying because you have never been able to do it in the past. So, you give up before you start, proving your Subconscious Mind is right. However, if you think that you can achieve your goal, the Subconscious Mind will search out any time you have reached your goal. Then you set out with high anticipation that you will be successful."

The last part of Dr. Fleet's Stickman is the Body. Although the Body is the most obvious part of you, it is also the smallest. The Body is the physical presentation of you. It is nothing more than an instrument of the mind. The thoughts or images that are consciously impressed on the Subconscious Mind must move the Body into action.

Actions you are involved in determine your results. The body looks solid, but if you looked through a powerful microscope, you would see that the body consist of tiny molecules that are constantly in motion. The body is a vibrating mass of energy. The Subconscious Mind sends out vibrations that the body picks up and you send out these vibrations, which cause your actions. Your actions cause reactions of others and this gives you your results. Results are your outcomes or consequences and effects of your actions.

Now we have a name for these vibrations. We call them feelings. Therefore, when you are in a positive form of vibration you don't say I am in a positive vibration today. No you say I am feeling good. Same goes that if you are in a negative vibration you say I am feeling bad.

This vibration attracts people and things to us. You attract what is in harmony with your paradigm. Negative people attract negative people. Positive people attract positive people.

It is important that you understand that the MIND is made of three different parts which work together to produce the results you are getting in your life. The thoughts you think and accept with your Conscious Mind will be impressed into your Subconscious Mind. The Subconscious Mind must accept every idea impressed upon it whether it is good or bad. The Body is the physical representation of the MIND and expresses your ideas and habits to the rest of the world.

"When you think about all the bad things that could happen to you, you are actually attracting these bad things to happen to you," I said as our lesson was winding down.

"So, every time I complain or worry about something bad happening to me, I am actually attracting it?" asked Kate.

"Yes that is exactly what you are doing," I replied. "Remember the story you told me earlier? It was your decision to be positive, that caused everything else to be positive that day. You attracted it."

"That is the end of today's lesson. Do you have any questions about the MIND?" I asked Kate.

"Just one, how do I control my thoughts and make sure that I stay positive?" Kate inquired.

"Excellent question." I replied with a smile. "Now you are aware of the damage negative thoughts can do. You will become more attentive to what and how you think."

"That's it? No special secret?" Kate said disappointed.

"I explained to you earlier awareness was one of the important parts of becoming successful. Now you are aware of how your mind works and you need to be alert to how and what you think about you are on your way to becoming successful," I explained. "Now, between now and the next time we get together I would like you to pay attention to every time you have a negative day. Write down what and how you were feeling that day. Can you do this for me?"

"Yes I can do that. And thank you for doing this with me. You are helping me more than I can tell you." Kate said with a smile.

"Don't mention it. It is my pleasure." I answered her.

CHAPTER 4

THE SIX INTELLECTUAL FACULTIES

"Reasoning is the mental tool that we use to think with."

Bob Proctor

Most people go through life dealing with and using only their five senses: See, Hear, Touch, Taste, and Smell. These are easy to identify as physical faculties. Many people rely on these five senses as the only supply they have for ideas. We look at grades in school, our bank account, or the economy and believe we cannot be successful.

However, the six intellectual faculties can be used to help create the success you are looking for. These intellectual faculties in no particular order are your Imagination, Intuition, Will, Memory, Reason and Perception. Many people don't understand these tools or how to use them. When they do use them they most times use them incorrectly. Developing these six Intellectual Faculties can help you achieve success.

I wondered how Kate was doing keeping herself positive. I was waiting for Kate at a local restaurant. It had been about two weeks, and I was eager to see her development. At our last meeting, she had shown so much growth. My lessons were beginning to gain traction in her Mindset. She was making positive improvements in her life. I couldn't wait to discover what Kate had been up to this week.

The restaurant door swung open, and Kate glided past the hostess. I waved her down as she made her way through the maze of tables and chairs. We were having a late lunch, so many of the tables were empty with dirty plates waiting to be collected. She sat down across from me with the server immediately following her. We ordered our meals, and while we waited, Kate was eager to ask me a question.

"So, am I ready to discover my dream - you know to set my goal that will help me find my purpose in life?" she asked as she squirmed to get comfortable in her seat.

"No, not quite yet," I answered. "First, I would like to ask you if you are still keeping a positive attitude?"

"I am trying," said Kate as she looked around the empty restaurant. "But, I do find myself getting negative now and then."

"That is to be expected," I told her. "I still have days when I get a bit negative. But I remind myself that I'm in control of my attitude. Now, how did you handle it?" I asked.

"It starts out the same as always. I get down and I feel bad about a situation, or something. Then I try to remember what you taught me...about choosing to be happy and positive," she shares.

"How did that work out for you?" I asked probingly.

"Well, before long, I start looking for the positive in situations." She continues with a smile on her face, "and you know what, you were right! Nothing is good nor bad until you decide it is. Once I made the decision to look for the positive, the bad stuff really isn't as bad as I thought. And a lot of the time I was reading too much into the situation."

"You know, there will always be times where it's harder than others," I reassured her. "I am proud of you. You are growing in awareness and as a person."

"So... am I ready now to discover my life's purpose and set my goal?" She inquired again.

"Almost," I responded. "But first, you must understand the mind a little bit more. You need to learn about your six intellectual faculties." "My six what?" She said puzzled.

"Your six intellectual faculties." I repeated.

Your six intellectual faculties are **REASON, PERCEPTION, WILL, MEMORY, INTUITION AND IMAGINATION**. These are very important when it comes to achieving your goals. Everyone has them, but few know how to use them. That's why some people never become as successful as they could be. These intellectual faculties are your mental muscles. Just like every other muscle, they can be strengthened with exercise.

"Beware, all too often we say what we hear others say. We think what we are told that we think. We see what we are permitted to see. Worse, we see what we are told that we see."

Octavia E. Butler

REASON: This is our thinking faculty and the ability to accept or reject an idea. It allows you to determine whether an idea you receive from others or developed by yourself is plausible. Whether you will accept it as truth or reject it as false.

You should spend time thinking for yourself. Use your own mind, reason with these ideas and decide whether to accept them or not. Do not just do this for what I'm teaching, do it for everything you hear, read and see.

To think for yourself is very hard work. Many people would rather just follow the crowd and take the easy route. You will find when you start thinking you will discover many times you just followed the crowd. If you had taken the time to think you would have never been a follower.

By taking the time to think and reason things out for yourself, you will begin to strengthen this mental muscle.

"Studies have shown that 90% of error in thinking is due to error in perception. If you can change your perception, you can change your emotion and this can lead to new ideas."

Edward de Bono

PERCEPTION: this is how you see the world not as it is but as you see it through your beliefs and habits.

If I put a 50-foot-long 12" wide plank on the ground and asked you to walk across it you would have no difficulty. Now, take the same plank, suspend it 4 feet off the floor and place a $100-dollar bill on one end and you would have little difficulty doing it. Again, take the plank, place one end on the edge of a 50-storey building. Place the other end on another building so the plank is suspended 600 feet in the air. Place $5,000 at the end. Would you walk across the plank to get the money? It would be more difficult. Why? The perception has changed. You would see the ground 600 feet below. Tiny people walking on the street. Your hair would be blowing in the wind and whistling past your ears. You already have proven to yourself you can walk across the beam when your life was not in danger. So, you know you can balance across the beam, your perception of the wood has changed. It is now 600 feet in the air.

You will come to realize that many things in the world change when you alter your perception. Things that seemed impossible are now easy. Try looking at situations a few different ways. You might be able to see something that you missed before.

"Willpower is the key to success. Successful people strive no matter what they feel by applying their <u>will</u> to overcome apathy, doubt or fear."

Dan Millman

WILL: is the power to concentrate.

To stay focused on one thing and block out all distractions. Concentrating thoughts can strengthen your vibrations attracting people and opportunities you need to achieve your goals.

Think of sitting in a dark room and you light a candle. The candlelight fills the room, but it is not too bright. Although there is light it is still difficult to see small details in the room like artwork or décor. Now, instead of candlelight you are equipped with a flashlight. Both have the same light energy, but the beam of the flashlight is more focused. When moving the torch around the focused light source, it illuminates the small details of the room. The rest of the space is still dark, but now you are able to more clearly see the artwork and décor. Your Will works in the same way. It focuses your attention on your goal.

"Kate, there are many distractions in our lives," I said. "Things standing in the way of your dreams such as your finances, people and wrong opportunities. Let me give you an exercise to help strengthen this muscle. It is an exercise to develop your power of concentration, Take a thumbtack and pin it to a wall across from your favorite chair. When you are alone and it is quiet, focus all of your attention on the pin. At first, you will be looking at the pin and your mind will drift to something else. Do not get discouraged. Bring your thoughts back to the pin. Keep doing this exercise until you can block out all other distractions. After a while, you will become one with the pin. It will take lots of practice to get to this stage, but don't give up. If you keep practicing, you will eventually get there."

"So, all I do is stare at a pin on the wall?" asked Kate "And I will strengthen my will?"

"That is it," I answered.

"That sounds stupid!" she practically stuck her tongue out at me while she said it.

"Well, try it and see if it's as easy as you think," I said, encouragingly.

I searched my bag for a pin that I brought anticipating this moment.

"Remember, if your mind drifts off the pin let me know. Let's see just how long you can concentrate." I challenged her.

"No problem." She said confidently

I stuck a pin in the wall across from where Kate was sitting and asked her to concentrate on it for as long as she could. After about ten seconds, Kate's mind started to drift. Her eyes started to droop. Her postured changed. I could tell her mind was starting to wander.

"Damn, I thought for sure I could concentrate longer than that," Kate said. I can't believe she confessed it.

"Most people are not used to concentrating," I said. "Ten seconds is not a bad start. Use this example and begin strengthening your will."

"I think that is enough information for one day." I told Kate.

"Yeah it's a lot to take in for one day." Kate replied

"Ok I will see you tomorrow and we can finish up

the last of the six intellectual faculties." I finished saying and got up and left.

"An educated person is a person who has so developed the faculties of their mind that they can acquire anything they want"

Bob Proctor

I wanted to get back together with Kate as soon as possible to finish the lessons on the six intellectual faculties. We decided her place was quiet enough for her to concentrate.

I arrived at her home. It was a modern building downtown close to the entertainment district. I pushed the buzzer and Kate let me in. She lived in a nice one bedroom apartment with a view of the city. Kate made me a coffee and we sat in the living room.

"Do you remember everything I taught you yesterday?" I asked.

"You taught me about the first three of the six intellectual faculties," she answered. "The first was REASON – and that I should practice by making sure I think for myself. Don't just follow the crowd."

"That's right, Never follow the crowd. Instead be like

the few going off on their own; they are thinking for themselves."

"Next was **PERCEPTION**," said Kate. "I need to look at my problems from multiple angles. That if I change my perception the problem may look different or not exist at all."

"Excellent way of putting it." I said proudly.

"The last one was **WILL** - my ability to focus. That I can increase my focus by concentrating on a pin and keeping my mind focused on it."

"You never realize what a good memory you have until you try to forget something."

Franklin P. Jones

"Let me start by asking you a question. Do you feel you have a good or poor memory? Could it be better? Are you forgetful?" I asked Kate.

"Now that you mention it my memory could be better." Kate said. "why do you ask?"

"What if I tell you everyone has a perfect memory? That with a bit of practice everyone can improve their memory." I replied.

"Really?" questioned Kate.

"Memory is the next intellectual faculty I want to teach

you." I answered.

Everyone has a perfect memory. When people say they have a poor memory they are actually giving power to what they don't want. People who don't remember things never took the time to memorize it in the first place.

"Would you like to learn a way to remember ten different things in just a few minutes?" I asked Kate.

"Definitely, it sounds interesting," she answered.

"You need a piece of paper and a pen. On the paper, write down the numbers one through ten. Beside one write run, beside two write zoo, beside three write tree, beside four write door, beside five write hive, beside six write sticks, beside seven write heaven, beside eight write gate, beside nine write wine and lastly beside ten write den. Now, say each set out load with me."

"One run, two zoo, three tree, four door, five hive, six sticks, seven heaven, eight gate, nine wine, and ten den," we said together.

"Now do it again with your hand on your chest so you feel the vibration each set makes," I said.

To be able to memorize certain things add ten different words that you want to remember. The trick to remembering is association. Not just any association, we use ridiculous association.

"Okay, so we need to use ridiculous association with the ten words I gave and the ten words that we first associated with the numbers," I began. "Beside one, you wrote pen and the word that goes with one run. Therefore, to help you remember pen we picture in our mind's eye a pen running around the room."

"Oh, I understand what you mean," she said between her laughter.

"Beside two you wrote book," I continued. "So, picture you and I walking through a zoo and as we walk you look into the monkey's cage and see a monkey reading a book. Three was watch. Picture a tree and in the tree instead of leaves you see watches. Four was calculator. Picture a calculator crashing into your front door. Five, which was hive and you wrote the word microphone. Now, picture a beehive with microphones all over it. Six you wrote cup. Picture trying to pick up a cup with chopsticks. Seven you wrote peanut. Picture peanuts flying around heaven with little angel wings on their backs. Eight you wrote soda-can. Picture a gate with soda-cans on it. Nine you wrote newspaper. Picture spilling a bottle of red wine on a newspaper. Last beside ten, you wrote paperclip. Picture opening the door to your den and a thousand paperclips are coming at you, so you slam the door."

I tested Kate's memory using ridiculous association. She remembered everything perfectly.

If you want to remember one hundred things, it's just as easy. All you have to do is chain the answers. Moving forward, eleven would chain with one and twelve would chain with two. To help improve your memory keep practicing this technique. You can increase the number of things you can easily remember all the way to one hundred.

"Your time is limited, so don't waste it living someone else's life. Don't be trapped by dogma – which is living with the results of other people's thinking. Don't let the noise of others' opinions drown out your own inner voice. And most important, have the courage to follow your heart and intuition."

Steve Jobs

INTUITION: this mental muscle is useful, but many people never give it much attention. This is your ability to pick up vibrations from other people and situations.

Have you ever entered a room and felt the tension? You knew that the people in the room were arguing. The vibrations from the people in the room were being picked up by your intuition. You knew something was not right. Many people have what they call a gut feeling. Some say they feel it in their heart. Others say they knew it in the back of their mind. Either way this is your intuition talking to you.

One day I was getting ready to leave my house. It was a warm and sunny day. Just as I was ready to go I got the feeling to grab a coat. I questioned myself as it was a beautiful clear day. However, I decided to follow my intuition and grab my coat. That afternoon it stormed and the temperature dropped. Although my friends made fun of me for bringing a coat, I was the lucky one after all. They were freezing and I was ready for the change in weather. I just had a feeling.

Using your intuition is quite easy. When you get a feeling to do something, do it. If you're walking down the street, come to an intersection and get the feeling to turn left. Do it. The whole point is for you to start trusting you. To start trusting your intuition. Pay attention to your intuition and start following it. See what opportunities it brings to your life.

"You can't depend on your eyes when your imagination is out of focus."

Mark Twain

IMAGINATION: this is the greatest gift humans were given. Everything created in the world is made twice. First in the imagination and then in the physical world. You can create in your imagination the future you want and see the dream you crave.

When we're young, we use our imagination all the time. We could be pirates, doctors, astronauts, or anything we could think up. As we get older we're told to stop daydreaming and pay attention. No more time wasting. Therefore, when we become adults our imaginations stop.

We usually negatively use our imagination. When your child is late coming home we start imagining a car crash, an ambulance or something worse.

What we need to understand is everything is a product of someone's imagination. Everything is created twice. First in imagination and second in reality. It's with your imagination you see your goals. See anything you could ever want. You have the mental muscle to create it in your mind.

"So, what good does it do me to only imagine what I

want in life?" asked Kate.

"Well, your imagination is the first part of the creation process," I explained. "Remember what I taught you. Everything that has ever been created by man was created twice." I said. "Well, by being able to imagine your dream you are taking the first step to creating it for real."

"So I need to be able to picture myself having my dream before I can actually make it come true." Kate answered. "Exactly!" I confirmed.

"Now before we get ahead of ourselves we have more work and training to do first." I explained. "Now have you been writing out things that you want in life as I asked you to do when we first started your journey."

"Yes." Kate answered. "I was going to ask you about that. Are we going to need them soon?"

"Yes please bring them with you to our next meeting." I replied. "We are ready to discover your dream and create your goal."

"Yes!" exclaimed Kate "I can't wait."

"Excellent see you in a few weeks." I said with a wink and huge smile on my face.

CHAPTER 5

CHOOSING THE PROPER GOAL WILL MOTIVATE YOU TO ACHIEVE IT.

"Don't set your goals too low. If you don't need much, you won't become much."

Jim Rohn

GOAL: The best way I know to describe a Goal, I learned from listening to Earl Nightingale. He described it as a ship with a captain and crew. Now give the ships' crew a destination, and plot a course how to get there. 9,999 times out of 10,000, the ship will reach its destination. Now take that same ship, this time don't give it a captain or crew. Don't give it a destination or set a course. Just start the engines and release it into the harbor. There is a high probability the ship will either sink or end up on a deserted beach as a derelict. People are just like a ship with a Goal, there is a high chance of achieving their dreams. Or they can go through life without a goal and hope that they don't crash or sink.

Everyone should set two types of goals. Firstly, long-term goals. These are goals that are achievable in the distant future.

Think of them as your dreams. Dreams motivate you to improve and give you hope for the future. Secondly, there are short-term goals. These are achievable daily, weekly or monthly.

Both types of goals tie together and help you to move closer to your dream. Write down both of these types of goals. It makes them permanent. This enforces them in your subconscious and makes them real. Write your dreams in a journal. A place where you can review them often. Also, you can track progress and cross-out completed short-term goals. Celebrate each goal you cross off. It will motivate you to achieve your dreams.

Most people have no idea how to choose a proper goal. One that will motivate you and keep you striving to achieve. It will cause you to grow as a person. It's important to choose a goal that's worth the effort to achieve it. Many people choose goals that are easily achievable. This limits growth.

I met Kate at the salon. While the owner was cutting my hair, she made a comment to me that I found interesting. She told me Kate seemed different.

"Different?" I asked. "How is she different?"

"Well, it's hard to describe, but she seems happier and more confident," the owner said.

"Really?" I said with a smile. "What makes you say that?"

"I don't know. She's smiling more and there just seems to be a different vibe from her."

"That's great!" I exclaimed.

"Whatever you're teaching her seems to be working. I am so happy for her."

"Have you told her any of this?" I asked.

"Oh...no."

"Why not?" I inquired.

"I don't know," she pondered while trimming my hair.

"Well, I think you should," I said. "It'll help build her confidence and let her know that people are noticing the changes in her."

"I will if you think it'll help."

"Oh, it will definitely help." I said.

After my hair cut and chat with the owner, I sat with Kate in the back room. It was quiet. We could talk without interruptions.

"If you think you're ready, it's time to choose your goal," I said. Kate's face lit up with excitement.

"Yes I feel ready to move forward." Kate replied.

"Before we start today's lesson, tell me what you have done to exercise your mental muscles."

"I have been practicing my concentration exercise to strengthen my Will," said Kate. "I think for myself. I make sure I look at situations from many angles to make sure I see the whole picture. I have practiced the memory game and actually taught it to my sister. But, I must admit that following my intuition and using my imagination hasn't been easy."

"There are people who always play it safe," I said. "They never tackle more than they can handle without effort or risk. By doing this they invite neither triumph nor defeat. They never learn the greatness of their mental ability or the strength of their endurance."

"How do I know if I chose a goal that is worthwhile?" asked Kate.

"If your goal scares you then you are on the right track," I started. "If you need to grow as a person then there's a good chance you have chosen the right goal. Make sure your goals are big and interesting enough to really fire up your emotions."

It's crucial you choose your goal yourself. Only you can decide what your goal is going to be. Many people will try to set your goals for you. Friends, partners, parents, employers or associates may offer suggestions. There is no one else who is capable of setting your goal but you. If they try, and they will, do not allow it to happen. Do not commit yourself to someone else's goal or one set to please someone else.

Your goals must be wants not needs. There is no inspiration in needs. There is inspiration in wants. Your goal does not have to be logical. Actually, you will probably be more inspired if it's actually illogical. The road to your goal will be a rough uphill battle. Therefore, it's important to be emotionally involved with the idea of reaching your goal. You need to have a burning desire and a love for what you want.

"Kate I am going to teach you a process on how to discover your goal based on a method taught to me by Bob Proctor. I want you to make out a want list," I told Kate. "You need to list 30 things you really want. Remember not needs, but wants. Be as specific as you can. For example, the house you'll live in, the job you want, or the places you'll travel to."

"Why is it so important to have 30 wants?" asked Kate.

"We will take your 30 wants and prioritize them. We will discover your A1 want. Or your most important and biggest want, we will use it to set your goals."

I gave Kate as much time as she needed to write her list. Her head was down at the table as she scribbled. Every so often she would look up to collect her thoughts and then get back to writing.

"Do you have your 30 wants?" I asked Kate.

"Yes," she answered. "It took longer than I thought it would to come up with 30. In the past, I never gave my wants much thought. When I forced myself to think about it I was surprised how hard it was to come up with 30 wants and not needs."

"It's time to start prioritizing them. Take some time to review your list and be sure you're happy."

Kate took some time to review the list. She crossed out a couple and added new wants. She placed the pen on the table, looked up and gave me a nod.

"Are you done?" I anxiously questioned.

"I think so," she said taking one last glimpse at the paper.

"Great, now it's time to start prioritizing. You need to put the 30 wants into three categories," I explained. "Categorize them as A, B or C wants."

"What if I can't decide whether it is an A, B or C?" asked Kate.

"Use your intuition," I told her smiling. "It'll guide you and keep you on the right track. Take as much time as you need."

I gave Kate time to finish categorizing her list.

"Now, it's time to prioritize again," I said.

"How do I do that?"

"Go through all your A's, B's and C's. Number them one

through ten. Again, use your intuition to help you choose the number for each want. Once you complete this task, I want you to write out three new lists."

"Alright, I'm excited to discover my goal," said Kate.

"Excellent, I'm glad to hear you're excited about your goal," I said. "Now that you have completed each list you will have your 'A1' want selected. This will be the starting point to creating your goal and the one to focus your attention on. You will find that most, if not all of the other wants will come as you move towards your A1 want. The other 29 will become stepping-stones on your journey to your goal. They can become short-term and long-term goals that help you reach your dream."

"What do I do now?" pondered Kate. "I have my A1 want, but it's not a goal yet."

"It's time to take your A1 want and write it out as a goal," I said.

Achieving goals is a creative process. The first step in the creation of your goal takes place in your conscious mind. Through your senses and imagination you must form a clear and concise image of yourself in possession of your goal. This image must be painted with words in as much detail as possible. Making a clear and concise written description of your goal will help clarify and crystallize the image in your Conscious Mind. You must be able to tell people about your goal and describe it in exact detail. It's important to own your goal on a conscious level.

Your image must be in the present and not the future. The mind only deals with the present. The moment you consciously entertain yourself in possession of your goal, you then have your goal on a conscious level. Begin thinking and talking like the person who has the goal. Consciously reaffirm your goal by rewriting your image as often as possible to strengthen the image in your mind.

"Remember to imagine yourself in possession of your goal," I told Kate. "This is when you get to use the intellectual faculty of imagination. Take as much time as you need to picture your goal in full detail. Then write out what you have pictured. Don't worry if it's not perfect. As we move forward in your journey, you will write it out many times. Each time more descriptive and clearer."

"I will give it a shot," finished Kate.

"Take as much time on this assignment as you need. It is very important that you spend all the time needed to imagine and write out your goal." I expressed to her.

"Because this is such an important part of your journey you will use this picture you've written in your next lesson."

"I promise to give this one hundred percent." Kate said. "I understand that this is important and I want to make you proud."

"Kate I know that you will do your best." I said. "Remember if you need any help at any time, just call or text me and I will do what I can to help you through the process."

"Thank you." Kate said with a smile, "I might just take you up on it."

"See you in three weeks."

CHAPTER 6

USING THE POWER OF VISUALIZATION TO HELP YOU ACHIEVE YOUR GOALS

"Visualize this thing that you want, see it, feel it, believe in it. Make your mental blue print, and begin to build."

Robert Collier

Visualize your goal. By seeing yourself in possession of your goal your Subconscious Mind will start to go to work for you, discovering ways to achieve what you visualize. The Subconscious Mind does this by attracting things into your life needed to achieve your goal. It'll change your focus so you start seeing the opportunities needed to move you towards your goal. Everything you need already exists in the universe, you need only to start to become aware of them. Having a clear picture of your goal creates a better chance of you achieving it. That's why it's important to take time every day to visualize your goal. Each time you do your goal becomes more defined. Always rewrite your goal after each time you spend visualizing it. To make sure you have a clear and precise written description.

This time Kate and I were meeting for coffee. The café was packed. There was a line up at the counter and no empty tables. I was hoping to find a quiet booth close to the back, but it wasn't looking good. After about 15 minutes two people left and a table was free. I grabbed it, sat down and waited for Kate. She came into the cafe and spotted me at my table. She walked over with a smile.

"Are you ready for today's lesson?" I asked as Kate sat down in the opposite chair. There were still some dirty dishes and used napkins from the previous occupants. Before Kate could get comfortable, a café employee came to clear the mess.

"Yes, I'm ready," said Kate. The server was balancing dishes on both arms trying to get out the way. "I'm ready to start my journey to achieve my goal," continued Kate. "Once I have it, I'll have everything I need. I'll be the NEW Kate and then I can be happy."

"Wait a minute," I said. "Don't fall into destination sickness."

"Destination sickness?" she asked.

"Yeah, destination sickness is the illness a person gets when they believe they will have instant happiness once achieving their first goal. You need to learn to be happy today and be grateful for what you have. Remember Kate," I continued. "A goal is a journey that you are on to grow and mature not a place to get to. It's the person you become while obtaining your goal that attracts success. Not the other way around."

"Oh," replied Kate. "I never thought of it that way. I always focused on getting the goal. I never thought about the person I was becoming along the way."

"Last time you prioritized your wants to get you to an A1 want. Did you get that finished?"

"Yes, I did all the work and used my intuition to prioritize the wants."

"Did you take the A1 want and write it out as a goal?" I continued. "Making it as descriptive as possible."

"Do you want to hear it?" she replied.

"Of course."

"My goal," Kate paused. "Is to go back to school to learn makeup techniques and skills used in movies, theater and-television. Afterwards get a job doing makeup in one of those industries."

"That's excellent," I said with a lot of pride.

I could see such progress in her attitude and confidence. She also looked proud of herself. It was a big life decision.

"Today, I'll teach you why it's important to visualize your goal and paint it even further into words," I said.

Now that you have established an A1 goal, it's vital to have a clear picture, in writing. Many people attempt their goal no more than once. Actually, most people never try to achieve anything. They decide it's too hard so they don't even try. Having your goal in writing greatly increases your chances of success.

It makes your goal real. A tangible thing you can see and touch. Take your goal. Build a picture of it in your mind. Imagine yourself in possession of it.

"Visualize yourself going to the school," I told Kate. "See yourself accepting your diploma. Use your imagination to picture these things in your mind." Kate concentrated. She thought and thought. Imagined and imagined.

"Yes, I think I see it," replied Kate.

"When you see it, make a written description of the goal. You should be relaxed. Remember to describe yourself as already having your goal."

When making a written description you are developing cells of recognition in your brain. Every time you think of your goal, these cells increase in amplitude of vibration. The image you have infused into the cells will flash in your mind. Your image must be as real in your mind as anything around you must. It's going to be turned over to your Subconscious Mind. Let it do all the work. Remember the Subconscious Mind only receives what you turn over to it. This is the spiritual side of your personality. Spirit always gives you an exact replica of the image you give to it. This is the Reciprocal Law that the spirit operates.

"Now, take some time to relax and imagine yourself in possession of your goal. Put it into words," I said.

"Okay, let me try," responded Kate.

After half an hour of imagining Kate came up with a goal. She wrote, "I am so happy and grateful now that I have graduated from the College of Makeup Art & Design. Also achieving an honors grade level and I am top in my class. I am enjoying the classes and teachers and made some longtime friends. I am receiving funding for school so that I did not have to go into huge debt."

"What do you think?" asked Kate.

"It's a great goal," I replied. "You started with something positive in your description and wrote a detailed image. Can you see yourself achieving this goal?"

"I can actually see myself receiving my diploma."

After writing your goal and have your picture imprinted into the cells of your brain. Take time each day to allow yourself to completely relax. Say your goal out loud. Picture yourself in possession of your goal. By doing this visualization exercise you are accomplishing three things. First, you cause your image to crystalize. Add missing parts until it's perfect. Second, put yourself in the vibration to attract what you desire. Third, become more comfortable with your new self-image. This enables you to live it every waking hour. After each visualization exercise, re-write your image in the present tense. Visualization gives energy to your goal.

"Really?" asked Kate. "I have to rewrite my goal every day? That seems over the top."

"Do it daily to crystalize it into your Subconscious Mind," I said.

"If I want to be emotional about my goal I need to see it?" questioned Kate.

"Exactly," I replied. "Every time you rewrite your goal, you will be able to describe how it makes you feel."

"If that's what it takes then I'll rewrite my goal every day," said Kate. "By the way, do you rewrite your goal every day?"

"Yes I do. I rewrite it in my journal every day." I said. "It is the first thing I do each morning. I also spend twenty minutes a day visualizing myself in possession of my goal."

"Really you spend that much time just visualizing it," Kate said surprisingly.

"I do." I replied, "I also make sure I act like the person in my goal. That way my Subconscious Mind works to help me achieve it."

"It does?" questioned Kate.

"Yes" I answered, "remember your Subconscious Mind wants to do everything in it's power to prove you right. So if I act like the person I want to be my Subconscious will help make it true."

"That's enough for today Kate. For the next few weeks make sure you take time to do your daily visualization of your goal. Then rewrite it out in as much clarity as you can."

"I will." Kate said, "I promise. Thank you."

Every time you do this you can picture your goal more clearly. You will start adding more detail to your picture making it more real. The clearer the picture gets in your mind the more you will be able to focus. As it crystalizes you become emotionally attached to your goal. You will be able to describe your goal with feeling. There will be excitement in your voice and cause others to be excited for you. Remember your goal is not something you are going to get. It's something you already **INTELLECTUALLY** and **EMOTIONALLY** have. It's only a matter of time until you have it **PHYSICALLY**.

CHAPTER 7

WHAT'S STOPPING YOU FROM ACHIEVING YOUR GOAL

"Move out of your comfort zone. You can only grow if you are willing to feel awkward and uncomfortable when you try something new."

Brian Tracy

The number of times people try before achieving their goal is less than one. It's less than one because most don't even try. Those who do try stop before they ever achieve it. Lots start with big intentions to achieve their goal, but many people stop just as fast as they start.

What is it that stops them? The Terror Barrier. It happens when people start to get emotional about their goals. When your Subconscious Mind starts warning you of all that could go wrong and why it's better to stay where you are. All your old habits and beliefs are stubborn. They fight back when threatened. You begin to have doubts about your abilities. These worries bring fear and anxiety. It's much easier to give up and remain the same. However, you can change your paradigm and no longer hit the Terror Barrier. Moving you forward towards your goal.

Two days after our last training session I received a text message from Kate. She was upset and feeling anxious. She was worried school was too expensive. Her concerns were being able to afford rent, bills and life if she wasn't working. How would she commute to the downtown Toronto school? I texted her back. I told her she was reaching the Terror Barrier. It was imperative to meet as soon as possible. The next day, we met at her apartment.

"What's a Terror Barrier? Asked Kate. She sat across from me. "How am I ever going to make this goal a reality with all of the issues?"

"Let me explain," I tried to calm her. "Then you'll understand all the feelings and worries you're experiencing."

"But, I don't see how this is will help me solve all my issues."

Kate was tearing a napkin into small and thin shreds. She was anxious. Although I helped her discover all these life changing goals, she was still scared of the worst case scenario. Kate expressed there were nights she couldn't sleep. She analyzed and over analyzed all the risks. Felt sick. Cried. The Terror Barrier was obvious.

"Just let me explain and it'll become clear," I said trying to ease her worries. "Now, what is it that makes us so reluctant to accept new ideas and move off into new directions? What is stopping you from achieving the goals you want? What makes us worry and feel anxious? Or stops us from taking the actions we need to achieve our goals. Why is it that so many people set out with good intentions, but never finish what they started? Or worse, not even try at all. This is what I mean when I say Terror Barrier."

The Terror Barrier is a scary thing. Some people actually make themselves sick with worry.

Let's start with the first stage of the Terror Barrier, referred to as Bondage. This is your starting position. A state you are in before you start any goal. X type represents your present thinking. You presently have X type thoughts. They are in harmony with your X type paradigm. This gives you X type results.

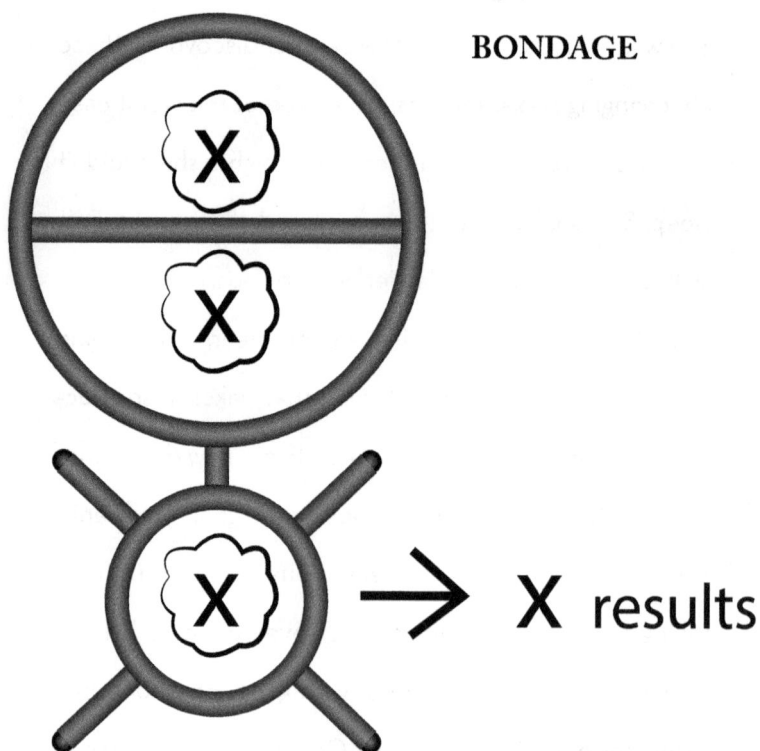

BONDAGE

X results

The second stage of the Terror Barrier is called Reason. This is where you created or heard a new idea. It's presented to the Conscious Mind. You can choose to accept or reject it. You're thinking about and reasoning with a new idea or the Y Type, but you haven't accepted it.

Similar to deciding on a goal. The idea is there to accomplish the goal. But, there's no acceptance to its possibility.

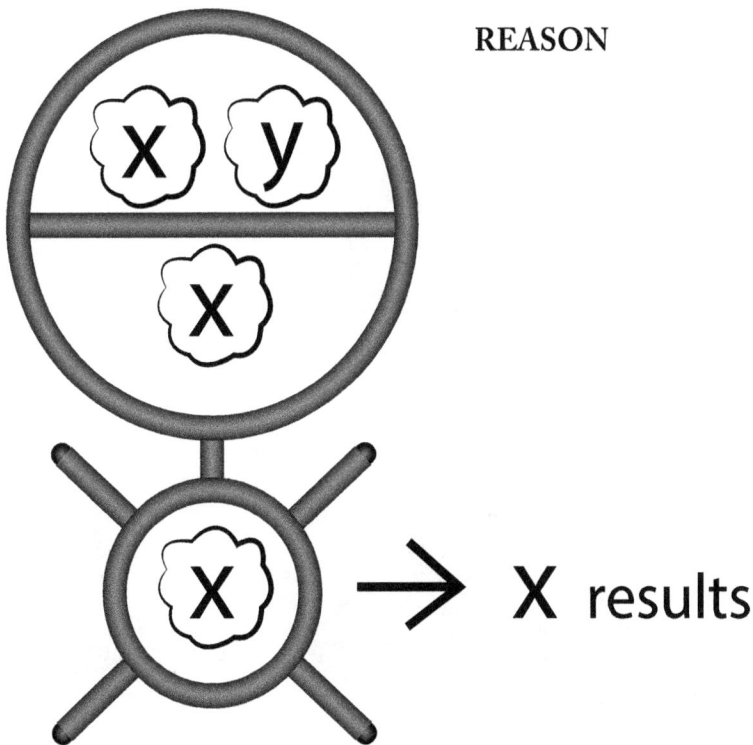

REASON

X results

Once we accept the idea, we move into the Terror stage. This is when you start to impress the new idea into your Subconscious Mind and get emotionally involved. Your Subconscious Mind is sending out foreign Y type vibrations that are strange and not in harmony with your normal X Type vibrations. These foreign vibrations are not in harmony with your paradigm. Therefore, this new idea causes you to have thoughts of doubt in the Conscious Mind. Causing fear in the Subconscious Mind leading to anxiety in the body. This is when you've reached the Terror Barrier.

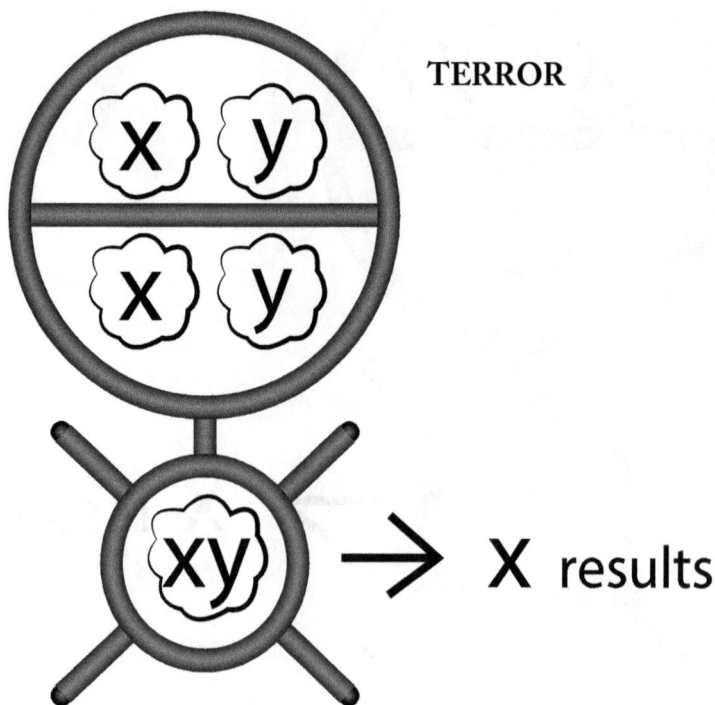

TERROR

$$xy \rightarrow X \text{ results}$$

"Now you started visualizing yourself actually having a goal," I continued, "you're getting emotional about it. You're accepting them into your Subconscious Mind and the vibrations are foreign. It's at this point many people give up their goals and go back to their comfort zone. People become trapped in the Bondage stage."

"How do I stop these feelings?" asked Kate. "What do I have to do to get passed the Terror Barrier?"

Most people need help crossing the Terror Barrier. The freedom stage is where you obtain the knowledge required to progress.

All through your life, coaches help you grow and reach your potential. Your parents helped you learn to walk, ride a bike and drive a car. Your teacher helped you learn to read and write, add and subtract. There have been many coaches throughout your life. The problem is most people finish school and believe they no longer need help in life. There needs to be a change in your paradigm. You must learn to accept the Y Type thoughts, cast off the X Type thoughts and cross from Terror Barrier into Freedom.

FREEDOM

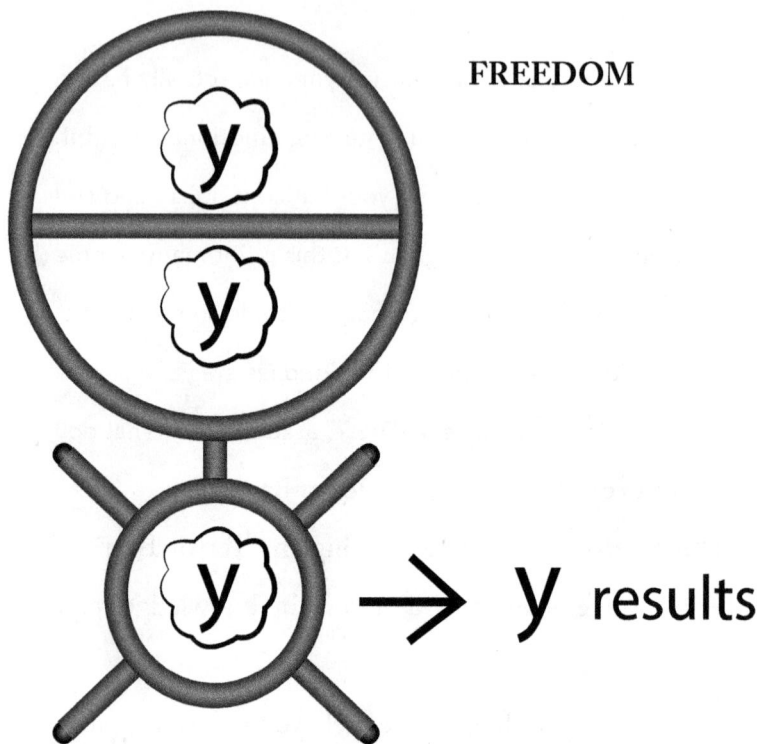

→ y results

The old X Type Ideas are replaced by the new Y Type Ideas. The vibrations are no longer foreign and doubt is gone. You are no longer anxious and you are now getting Y Type Results.

"Kate, I'm your coach," I said. "I'll give you the skills to cross the Terror Barrier and coach you along the way."

"What do I need to learn to cross the Terror Barrier?" asked Kate.

"Let go of the Past," I enthusiastically said. "It's time to learn how to change your old paradigm. The one holding you back from achieving your goals."

"How do I change my paradigm asked Kate?"

"That lesson is for our next meeting." I replied. Think about what I have taught you here. We will get together very soon."

When I left Kate I knew she was still worried and anxious, but I also knew that she would use her reasoning ability to think through what we had discussed.

CHAPTER 8

YOU CAN CHANGE YOUR PARADIGM

"If you want small changes in your life, work on your attitude. But if you want big and primary changes, work on your paradigm."

Stephen Covey

By learning how to change your paradigm, you can learn how to move forward and achieve your goal. Your paradigm is a multitude of ideas fixed in your Subconscious Mind referred to as habits and beliefs. To change your paradigm begin giving it new fixed ideas. Do this through the power of autosuggestion. Autosuggestions are positive ideas imprinted on your Subconscious Mind in the form of affirmations. Positive statements said repeatedly with feeling. Say affirmations in the morning when you first wake up and at night before you fall asleep. It is at this time your Subconscious Mind is best suited for new ideas.

Kate was going through a rough time hitting the Terror Barrier on her journey. I decided I should continue her lessons here and now at her apartment. A place she felt safe to talk openly.

"Are you feeling any better then?" I started by asking. "I feel a little better," she responded. "However, I'm still very anxious and have no idea how I'm ever going to achieve this huge goal."

"If your goal doesn't scare you then it's not right for you. The purpose of a goal is to make you grow. It's not what you get by achieving your goal, but rather who you become. The fact that you're scared and anxious means the goal you have picked is a good one. The person you will become by achieving it will surprise you."

"Okay, then how do I start to grow and become an impressive person?"

"We need to change your paradigm," I answered.

Your paradigm has your mind set at a certain frequency like a radio. You can only hear the music playing on that frequency, or in this case, you can only see the opportunities and possibilities on this frequency. By changing your paradigm you'll learn to alter the frequency you're listening to. When you do that, you will start to hear and see new opportunities and possibilities. They were always there. Your paradigm is stopping you from seeing them. You're not picking up the frequency yet.

"Teach me how to change my paradigm. I want to start working on achieving my goal," said Kate.

"Start by understanding the best way to impress your Subconscious Mind. Through the power of Autosuggestions," I responded. "They are the images and ideas impressed by you on the Subconscious Mind. These images and ideas become part of your paradigm."

Through the power of Autosuggestion, your image is being

properly deposited in the treasury of the Subconscious Mind. When the image of your goal is planted it's not only automatically expressed through your body in vibration and action, but affects everything in harmonious vibration with it. This is called the Law of Attraction. As we covered this in Chapter 2, your firmly planted image sets in motion a magnetic force to attract into your life all that's in harmony with it. To impress these images we use affirmations. Or positive statements that describe a desired situation or goal repeated until they get impressed on the Subconscious Mind. This process causes the Subconscious Mind to strive and work on your behalf and make the positive statement come true.

Most people repeat negative words and statements in their mind. Words work in two ways either to build or destroy. The way we use them determines whether they're going to bring good or harmful results. Your Subconscious Mind accepts anything as true. It attracts corresponding events and situations into your life. Therefore, choose only positive statements in order to get better results.

At any given moment, we're constantly bombarded by signals from at least four of the five senses. The visual system is constantly processing our surroundings. All of the many miniscule sounds that compose our environment stimulate the auditory system.

We are taking in all the smells around us and we're constantly feeling the clothes on our skin.

Within one sensory system there's an enormous amount of data being processed. We pay attention to only a small proportion of the information and throw much of it away. This process is known as selective filtering or attention. Most people do it all the time. Imagine watching a movie at a theater. If you're focused on the film you're probably not noticing the sound of squeaking seats, crunchy popcorn, or air conditioning.

"Think about before you bought your car," I said. "I'm sure you didn't notice many of them on the road. You probably weren't sure if anyone else drove one. But, when you bought the car you saw the same model everywhere."

"That's so true," replied Kate. "After I got my car, everywhere I drove I saw the same car. Sometimes even the same color."

"You changed your frequency. The things your mind focuses on. The cars were always there. You just didn't focus on them."

CREATING AN AFFIRMATION

- First, start by setting a positive feeling and attitude e.g. I am so happy and grateful.

- Second, you must state your affirmation in the present text e.g. now that.

- Third, you must make your demand to the Universe e.g. I am attracting to me.

- Fourth, have big wants and dreams, be specific e.g. health, wealth and success.

- Fifth, give it a time line or a permanent situation e.g. in to my life today.

- Finally put it all together and say it with feeling and belief e.g. I am so happy and grateful now I am attracting health, wealth and success into my life today.

Repeat this to yourself each morning when you first wake up and every evening before you fall to sleep

"I need to create positive affirmations," said Kate. "Then say them out loud each morning and night. So I will impress the positive idea into my Subconscious Mind."

"That's correct," I replied. "Each time you do the exercise it changes your paradigm and sends out vibrations attracting the right things. You will start seeing opportunities needed to achieve your goal. Now, try creating a few affirmations."

"Alright, I think I can do that." Kate thought for a few minutes intermittently jotting down ideas. This is what she came up with:

I am so happy and grateful now that I am attending makeup school.
I am so happy and grateful now that I have the money to pay for school.
I am so happy and grateful now that I am getting honor grades at school.

"Are these affirmations good enough?" asked Kate.

"An excellent start," I told her. "As you move towards your goal, you'll discover new affirmations to help change your paradigm."

The mind filters out millions of pieces of information. Otherwise you could never manage all the things coming at you. Changing your paradigm will shift what you're focused on. This way you'll be able to see the opportunities to achieve your goal. By repeating your affirmations to your Subconscious Mind, you are altering your filter settings of your frequency. It's up to you to pursue these opportunities.

CHAPTER 9

ACHIEVING YOUR GOAL

"Setting a goal is not the main thing. It is deciding how you will go about achieving it and staying with that plan."

Tom Landry

Achieving a goal is a three level creative process.

The first level is intellectual - The moment you started thinking about your goal. Visualizing it and writing it out. You can describe it to other people.

The second level is emotional - When you begin to have feelings about it. When you describe how your goal makes you feel.

The third level is physical. After some time you will have it on the physical level.

No one has the awareness of how long it takes a nonphysical seed to become a physical goal. But, it happens.

When Kate arrived for her lesson she was excited with something important to tell me. She has started to sell a few paintings at different art events. Things were starting to become a reality. Kate was scared of the unknown, but excited by visualizing her future. And becoming an amazing person who believed in the power to change her life. Kate's blossoming art career wasn't all she had to share with me.

"I have so much stuff I want to talk to you about," exclaimed Kate. "I started saying my affirmations each morning when I wake up and just before I fall asleep."

"What has that done for you?" I asked.

"Well, I started researching schools and found the perfect one. I went for a tour and it's amazing. I filled out all the forms and now I'm waiting to find out if I'm accepted."

"That's wonderful! I'm so proud of you!"

"That's not all," continued Kate. "I also found out that I can apply for funding from the government. If I get it, I don't even have to pay it back. Isn't that amazing?"

"It truly is. What do you need to do to get this funding?"

"Well, there are many forms and I need to be out of work for three months before I can apply. So, I can't actually apply for another two months, but this could be the answer."

"This is great news. I'm happy you're seeing new opportunities," I said. Kate was so excited. I could see an undeniable change in how she has gone about things. Her goals were starting to materialize and she was seeing the opportunities needed for success.

"Also, I looked into a student loan and talked to my family about it," she went on. "My mom told me if I really needed to, I could borrow the money from her. I would rather get it from other sources though."

"Why?" I asked.

"Well I don't want to put anybody else out so I can have my dream. I really want to do this myself."

"That is very responsible of you Kate. You're growing and maturing more and more each time I see you."

"Thanks," said Kate "Now I've written my goal and spent time visualizing each day. How much time do I give myself to reach my goal?"

"This is a very common question," I said. "No one has ever developed the awareness of how long it takes a non-physical seed to manifest. You must guess."

"How can I guess?"

The process of creation was also taught to me by Bob Proctor . The moment you consciously entertain the image of yourself in possession of your goal you have it on the first level of creation (intellectual). You have created a non-physical seed. You then plant the image (non-physical seed) in the proper environment – your Subconscious Mind, and let yourself get emotionally involved with the image of your goal.

The moment you get emotionally involved with your goal, the image instantly and automatically begins to move into physical form. The common error most people make when guessing at the time it will take to reach the goal is that they give themselves too much time. People have a hard time estimating what they are capable of accomplishing. They over estimate how much they can do in a day. Under estimate how much they can accomplish in a week. When it comes to a big goal people will estimate a huge amount of time to achieve it.

The Law of Gender decrees that all seeds have a gestation period before they manifest in form. We understand the non-physical seeds (ideas) are subject to this same law. When it comes to physical seeds we become aware of the length of time for gestation. We know if we plant wheat in the Spring by Fall it will be ready to harvest. However, no one has the awareness of how long it takes a nonphysical seed to become reality. You have to take your best guess. Never change the goal. Change the time. Change the plan. But, keep focused on the goal. If the time you gave yourself has passed, change it. If the actions you're taking are not bringing you closer to your goal, you need to change your plan. By taking the actions required, you will receive your goal on the third level of creation or the physical level.

In every good book there are countless stories of people with great purpose and high ideals. They worked hard towards and finally reached remarkable goals. These people came up against barriers and circumstances that would have stopped most people. What was it that kept them going, to forge ahead when things got tough? How were these people able to do what the average person would not even attempt? **BELIEF**. It was unshakable. No one or thing could destroy their unshakeable **BELIEF**. Everyone is blessed with the same abilities.

You must develop your **BELIEF** based on understanding. Their faith was not blind. It had strong foundation based in understanding. It was not difficult for them to Believe, because they knew and understood their role in the creative process. You must believe that you can achieve your goal. It's this belief in yourself that will keep you going when times get hard. When others tell you to give up.

When you believe that you can achieve your goal, you will achieve it. When you believe you can achieve your goal then you will have it.

The next important part of achieving your goal is a burning Desire. The Image of your Goal properly planted and constantly nourished with positive, expectant thought-energy will cause your goal to develop into a burning desire. This desire will cause you to take action to obtain your goal. Without the desire to achieve your goal you will easily give up when things get difficult. The burning desire fires your passion and keeps you moving towards your goal.

"So, I need to really want the thing I'm after," said Kate. "That's why you made me go through the whole exercise of writing out my want list. You wanted me to choose the right goal. The one that I would desire."

"Yup," I replied. "Kate, I want you to write your goal on a card. Carry it loosely in your pocket or purse touching it often. This card is only a symbol. When you touch it the cells of recognition in your brain will be triggered. The image of your goal you've been visualizing will flash on the screen of your mind. The picture you hold in your mind will eventually be expressed in physical form or circumstance. Follow your feelings and take each step ahead towards your goal. You'll quickly become aware of the changes taking place in your conditions, circumstances, and environment. Through reason you'll adapt to these changes and a new awareness will form in your mind. You'll see the next step to your goal."

"So, you're saying that I'll have a feeling of what I should be doing?" asked Kate.

"That's right. You've already experienced this, but didn't

realize it. How did you pick the school that you wanted to attend?"

"Well, I was searching the internet, found their website and looked into it."

"Why did you decide to search the internet?"

"I felt if I wanted to achieve the goal I set for myself I better start looking for a school to attend."

"You felt like you should look into a school?" I questioned.

"Yes," she answered. "I felt like I should. Oh wait, I see what you mean. I followed my feelings."

"That's correct. You were using your intuition."

"Now I understand why you taught me about the mind and all the stuff about my intellectual faculties. I've been using them all along. I didn't even realize I was doing it."

I smiled and nodded. "You're using your Reasoning faculty as we speak," I continued. "Without higher awareness, which developed because of the changes you have made, you wouldn't be able to see the next step. The good people wish for is always here. They're just not aware of it."

CHAPTER 10

DAILY OBJECTIVES KEEP YOU MOVING FORWARD

"If you don't have daily objectives, you qualify as a dreamer."

Zig Ziglar

Your daily routine determines how successful you will be. It's important to take a look at what you're doing on a daily basis. Set daily objectives that you strive to achieve each day. They don't have to be huge, but they must move you closer to your goal. Take a good hard look at your day. How much time are you wasting? What could you be working on? What books should you be reading? What people should you be meeting? What courses and seminars should you be attending? All of these things will help you reach your potential and obtain your goal.

This was the longest time between our sessions. I hadn't seen Kate for a few weeks. My phone rang.

"Randy, guess what happened," it was Kate on the other end.

"What?" I asked.

"They accepted me into the school I was hoping for."

"That's excellent news. Tell me everything."

"Well, a few weeks ago I told you I found the perfect school online. I went for a tour of the college. I loved everything," said Kate. "Oh Randy, it's amazing. The classes, the teachers, the whole facility. I took an application home and filled it out. There was a lot of information, but I stuck to it. I just heard back yesterday that I've been accepted.

Isn't that amazing?"

"It's great news," I replied. "Are you excited?"

"I am, but at the same time I'm scared and very anxious."

"Why do you think you're feeling like that?"

"I know this was my goal, to go to a great school to learn about makeup and special effects. However, I'm not sure how to pay for it. I haven't applied for the funding money yet. What if I can't afford it or I'm no good at it."

"Slow down," I said trying to calm her down. "What have you learned about these feelings you're experiencing?"

"I'm hitting the Terror Barrier again aren't I?"

"Yes. So, what do you need to do to cross over this Terror Barrier?"

"I need to change my paradigm," she answered. "I need to create some new affirmations to help me change my frequency. That way I'll be able to see the opportunities that are out there for me."

"That's correct," I said with a big smile. "Kate, you've matured so much over the past few months. I see before me now a confident and assured young woman where once stood a scared child. I have a few more things to teach you. Let's get together tomorrow."

"Okay, that works. I'll see you tomorrow," said Kate as she hung up the phone. I had never been more excited to meet. Everything was coming into place. She was finally starting to make connections between the lessons.

When I saw Kate the next day I gave her a big hug. We met at the same coffee shop we've been coming to since the beginning. It became our special place. Tables were empty and employees chatting behind the counter. The burnt smell of coffee filled the air. We sat down across from each other.

"Kate, first I want to go through a list of everything you've accomplished," I said. "You have chosen a goal. You consciously built a mental image of your goal. You made a written description of the mental image of your goal. You then planted that image in your Subconscious Mind. You nurtured that seed with positive thoughts and actions until it became reality. Be proud of yourself. You've proven to be a person that gets things done."

Kate adopted an entirely new routine designed to optimize her time towards achieving her goals. There was a positivity developing around her that radiates. She looks happier, healthier and confident. The positive changes in her were apparent. Happiness is something you choose to feel. There's still work to be done. Days where anxiety is overwhelming. But, Kate has grown so much. She was controlling her thoughts and focused on the future.

"So, I'm a successful person by setting goals and plans to achieve them?" asked Kate.

"Precisely," I answered. "You'll find people who have a clearly defined goal, made a list of objectives for each day and didn't let others distract them. They're not busy for the sake of being busy. They're working effectively on things that'll benefit them in achieving their goals."

"How many things should I have on my list?" questioned Kate. "How do I know if I'm choosing the right things to do?"

"Ask yourself this, am I bringing myself closer to my goal or further away?" I said. "It's that easy. If I want to lose ten pounds should I choose a healthy salad or a delicious cheeseburger?"

"Uhhh...the salad," replied Kate. "Yes, when it comes to knowing what action to take in life, I need to think whether or not it's bringing me closer or further from my goal. I get it. Only make decisions that work towards my goal."

"Exactly," I said. "Now, the other question you asked me

was about the amount of objectives on your daily to-do list. You should have six to complete each day."

"I need to make a list of the six things to do each day and prioritize them. Then do them in the order I chose."

"That's it. Understand that successful people develop an awareness. It allows them to detect those objectives that are goal achieving and call for instant attention. Then act on them until they're completed. Also, successful people are rarely rushed, and in a panic. People without goals seem to always be in a hurry. Individuals who don't have a goal experience this when they have lots to do. Also, they cause misunderstanding and confusion. Successful people always have lots to do. However, they know they can do it and complete work in calm confidence."

"Well, that makes sense," said Kate. I could feel our lesson was winding down. The coffee shop was starting to close. Employees were putting chairs on the tables and wiping the counters. Kate started to put on her jacket.

"Remember one thing," I said. "Stay positive, believe in yourself and you can do anything you set your mind to."

Kate got up. I watched her leave with more confidence and the knowledge of how to achieve her goals.

CHAPTER 11

CONCLUSION

"Life isn't about finding yourself. Life is about creating yourself."

George Bernard Shaw

The world always needs individuals who can get things done. People who are self-starters. People who see a task through to the end. It's not how much you know, but what you get done. The world rewards and remembers. The biggest handicap to your success is not a lack of brains, character, or willingness. It's the desire to get things done. Many people are held back from success. People who fail to do something great almost do it on time. They almost get the promotion. They almost become leaders. They never invested the time and energy to choose a goal that gives direction to their life. These people aren't lazy. They're busier than effective people. They mess around all day and all night. Indecision holds them back. A lack of planning and spending too long on minor things. You don't have to work harder. Just more effectively. You must learn to make your work count.

Update on Kate:

She attended the school of her choice. Where she was one of the top three in her graduating class. She made the Dean's List and many great friends. Just as she had visualized in her goal. Some of the people she met are in the movie industry. They are helping her make contacts for the future.

She is pursuing her painting and has been showing her artwork at a monthly event. She had a few of her paintings featured in the local art gallery.

The future looks extremely bright for Kate and she is an inspiration to all the people in her life.

Our hope is that you found this book very helpful and useful. Here are more offers from Randy Drake and The Randy Drake Team.

PROGRAMS

The Three Key Ingredients to Your Success

Working with people wanting to become more and achieve more. The Randy Drake Team teaches skills and gives tools that help you earn more money, build your business, and help you achieve your dreams.

We do this by focusing on these key ingredients:

We work on your Mindset; your beliefs and habits. We help you to remove limiting beliefs and habits that are acting like blinders stopping you from seeing opportunities that are out there.

A shift in habits and beliefs will lead you to set Goals to achieve these new opportunities. We will help you in the setting of these goals, ones which will move you with purpose towards your success.

However, for these goals to work, you need the last ingredient Plans. Plans, which will turn your dreams into reality and not only wishes.

WORKSHOPS

Learn How to get Anything you want in Life One Day Workshop
Our workshop is developed with you in mind. Helping you to discover your goals and then putting them to the test to make sure it is real. Helping you to succeed in life. We help to develop your conscious awareness that will move you closer to achieving your goals.

KEYNOTE SPEAKING

Is your company, group or conference looking for an insightful, dynamic and informative keynote speaker for your next event? Randy Drake will educate & entertain your audience. Randy Drake is a certified Coach, Trainer and Speaker who is passionate about helping others achieve their goals and dreams. Through his keynote speeches, Randy will explain the reason why most people never get to experience the success that they long for and strive to achieve.

For more information, please visit our website at:

www.randydraketeam.com

Stay informed click on the subscribe link on our website and get the RANDY DRAKE Team Newsletter monthly.

www.ingramcontent.com/pod-product-compliance
Lightning Source LLC
Chambersburg PA
CBHW061743020426
42331CB00006B/1344